Your Firm
Everywhere
Now

HOW TO POSITION YOUR PROFESSIONAL
SERVICES FIRM AS AN AUTHORITY IN
YOUR MARKETPLACE, INCREASE YOUR
ONLINE PRESENCE AND GENERATE MORE
BUSINESS.

Michael Alf

totalu Pty Ltd.
Melbourne, Australia

Michael Alf / totalu Pty Ltd.
8 Bowman Street
Aspendale, 3195 VIC, Australia
www.yourfirmeverywherenow.com
E-Mail: contact@totalu.com.au

Ordering Information:
Quantity sales. Special discounts are available on quantity purchases by corporations, associations, and others. For details, contact the "Special Sales Department" at the address above.

Your Firm Everywhere Now / Michael Alf. —1st ed.
ISBN 978-1506142777 (Createspace)

Contents

Dedicated to Andrea

"A mind needs books as a sword needs a whetstone, if it is to keep its edge."
— George R.R. Martin, *A Game of Thrones*

Acknowledgement

"There is a book in everybody."

I believe it is true and I think there is actually much more than one book in each of us. After a couple of years we have all experienced so much in life, went through so many lessons - some harder some easy. And we collected a lot of relevant knowledge, which could help other people.

But usually putting a book out is also a lot of work and so you need support from other people. The same is true for me even though I am now helping individuals to become published - best-selling - authors. That is why I would like to acknowledge some of the people who helped me along the way.

The first two individuals are Ed Rush and Mike Koenigs. Mike and Ed created not only the Publish & Profit system, which this book is partially a result of, but I have also learned a lot of them in the last 15 months alone. Truly focused on their clients with exceptional creativity and passion they both are impacting the world in a positive way. Mike was also the person who triggered the title based on his own book "You, Everywhere, Now."

Then a special thank you to Pam and Chris Hendrickson - also from San Diego - and Jeanne Hurlbert. They created the marketing roadmap based on their extensive experience and I had the great pleasure to not only go through the course but also get certified so I am now able to work with clients here in Australia and in other countries. Chapter 10 is heavily impacted by their work.

Damien Zamora from GoMobile and his team had impact on all mobile aspects of the book and I am thankful for all the learnings I got from him in the last 15 months.

The many members of the Publish & Profit community with all their valuable real-time feedback - not the least about the cover, the title and subtitle and the colours.

There are many more people who have had some influence or impact on the book - so when you know me in person you might have had some impact as I believe we are who we are based on all the single interactions with multiple other individuals and we never know which idea or thought was initiated by which conversation.

And of course lastly I would like to thank my wonderful wife Andrea and my daughters Katharina and Franziska for all the support they provided. I am truly blessed to have such an amazing family.

CHAPTER 1

Why This Book and Why Me?

Dear friend, welcome to my book, Your Firm Everywhere Now. Before we start together diving into the content, I would like to give you a summary and an overview of what you can expect in this book going forward.

I would also like to briefly introduce myself so that you know who actually is writing the book, and who you are interacting with and talking to in the book.

I started my professional career many, many years ago with the armed forces in Germany. I joined the officer's career and, then, became responsible for IT and the establishment of communication channels in various air defence groups. So, at that time, I was already in the services industry. I was basically servicing the other units to help them communicate, exchange data, and fulfil their mission. And that has become a theme throughout my journey and throughout my life - to serve and help others achieve what they want to achieve. This is what I'm passionate about.

Then, after 10 years, I left the armed forces as a captain and decided to join one of the largest consulting and IT companies in the
world. I joined them in Germany where I lived at that time. That
was in 1999.

As is common for senior consultants, I started in project management, implementation work, process reengineering, and so on,
and then quickly moved into the area of account management. In
this role, I was dealing with customers all the time. I then developed
an approach for large (global) account management. My key client,
at the time, was a major player in the logistics area.

So, again, I was a service provider working in a service-based
business and serving another service provider. That allowed me to
uncover common threads and themes, which turned out to be very
beneficial later on.

After a number of years with work across the board from HR,
procurement, finance, marketing and sales, strategy, and operations,
I then had the opportunity to move to Melbourne in 2008.

So, my family and I packed the bags. On our trip to Melbourne,
we actually had to leave back one suitcase because of overweight.
We landed in the middle of summer in December 2008 in Melbourne.

We landed just when the global financial crises hit the world, so
it turned out to be a challenging time - new country, new language,
new colleagues, new market.

Over a period of three years, I have made some great progress.
We won and delivered interesting projects and grew the organisation significantly. But, I also discovered my passion for Internet and
online marketing. So, I started investing and learning, and I made a

lot of mistakes - even some big mistakes. That meant that I also learned a lot during this time. I tried out what works (hardly anything at that time) and what doesn't work, and I tested out various things. And when I left - officially it was a mutual separation - I tried to utilise some of that knowledge in the marketplace - with little success.

So, I got another role in a logistics company running the project management office.

But, I kept on dreaming and thinking of my own digital marketing business. And, of course, this led to another separation. I decided to take things seriously and build my own digital marketing agency. I initially started out with a focus on law firms only.

What I discovered was that it is a very interesting industry and, yes, there is a big need with regards to marketing and digital marketing. But, it also seems there is not that level of urgency that makes it really viable. Later, I found a great quote from Nick Abrahams, who is a partner at a Sydney legal firm and calls himself a "legal futurist". He compared lawyers with a frog in a pot that is slowly being brought to the boil, comfortably numb.

You might know this story of the frog and the boiling water. So, when you have a pot of water and you have a frog in there and you boil the water up, the frog typically won't jump out of the water and will miserably die in the water. Though, when you actually take a frog and throw it into boiling water, the frog immediately jumps out and survives.

So, Nick Abrahams is saying that his perspective on the legal industry is that they are more the frog in the water which is actually boiled. And what is boiling the water? Well, it's all the trends and the developments in the marketplace and the things that are changing so quickly. Many of those we are covering in this book.

But, the challenge, obviously, is that the frog in the water doesn't have the urgency and isn't willing to pick up new things.

I know there are many positive exceptions, and you might be one of them. But, those are exceptions and not the average.

So, I decided to broaden my focus on professional services' firms in general because I recognised that I already had a number of clients in this field (law firms, financial advisers, accountants and consultants).

Looking at the busy and noisy market today, one key question becomes how to differentiate you and how to position yourself as an authority to gain more clients and customers. One of the strongest positioning instruments - and I'll talk about that in the book - is a book, your book.

The book you are reading right now is basically a proof of how positioning works, and it is actually one of our key offerings we help individuals and businesses with. We have developed and adopted a proven five-step process that allows you to get a book - usually a top-10 best-seller - with a limited time investment of a couple of hours (sometimes as little as five).

Why the title, Your Firm Everywhere Now? It is adopted from Mike Koenigs' best seller, "You, Everywhere, Now", who explains and talks about how to use various ways to position yourself. Mike Koenigs is a serial entrepreneur and seven-time #1 best-selling author. I took his concepts, transferred it to firms and businesses, and added some new aspects.

Let's talk briefly about what you can expect from this book now that you have an idea how I decided to write it.

The idea of the book is to give you a good overview of what is working today and what is not working today. It's meant to be a very practical guide with advice you can implement straight away into your firm. It's, therefore, written in a very casual and hopefully easy to understand way, and it's straight to the point. It's short and sharp so that you can probably get through it in something like two hours or so. It's structured in a way to give you an understanding of why things are important, and to give you ideas about what you could do in your firm. And then, probably most importantly, I am closing with Chapter 10 about how you actually get started, where I talk about the marketing roadmap concept. This concept lets you develop a marketing roadmap for your organisation that takes out a lot of the overwhelm and gives you a clear focus in your marketing efforts. The roadmap contains what to do, which content to focus on, which products and services to focus on, and how to integrate all of it into a cohesive marketing plan.

So, this is what the book is about. I hope you enjoy it. I would appreciate your feedback and questions. It is interactive, where I give you the opportunity to get even more content, or ask specific questions, and you can get in touch with me. And, if you find an error or spelling mistake or something like that, I would very much appreciate an email so we can correct this (contact@totalu.com.au).

The book is not written to be a New York Times best seller or to win a Pulitzer Prize because I wanted to deliver something that helps you in your firm or in your business. In that sense it is a business book with a focus on the WHAT versus the HOW.

So, enjoy the book and let's get started.

Your Clients Are Online - are you?

I t takes 26 hours to report a lost wallet and it takes only 68 minutes to report a lost phone.

In this chapter, we talk about why online and digital marketing is so relevant today - and more than ever before. I will provide a lot of relevant and maybe surprising statistics and information, which will provide you a better view and perspective in understanding what's happening right now in the marketplace.

Your clients are online. Let me, firstly, share with you how businesses are seeing the marketplace at the moment and the marketing priorities and focus areas.
And, then, the second focus is mobile as you can see from the statistic above.

So, let's talk about the areas of interest firstly. The top three marketing priorities are (Source: ExactTarget, 2014 State of Marketing Survey):

For 47% of businesses, driving increased conversion rates is a top priority.

46% are saying an increase and improvement of the brand awareness is top.

And 29% are seeing the collection, measuring, and eventual using of behavioural-based data as very important.

That's why this book is called Your Firm Everywhere Now, which is obviously mainly around an increase in brand awareness through positioning and also driving higher conversion rates. So, it really addresses the top two things.

Let's now look at digital marketing priorities and let's look at the top four priorities here.

Top number one is commerce or e-commerce experiences. That is, of course, less relevant for professional services firms.

Then, social marketing is the next on the list. That applies to professional services firms as well, and is regularly misunderstood.

The third one is content creation and management. We'll talk about that in the book, and about the new ways of content marketing. Again, this book is an example for content creation and management.

And, then, the fourth item is, not surprisingly, mobile marketing. We'll talk about that in a moment as well.

Now, let's move to the spending trends. One of the top areas in which businesses invest at the moment is marketing and lead generation. Within that area, there are five top areas for increased spending:

The first one is "data & analytics," which is increasing for 61% of businesses.

60% are investing more into marketing automation, and we cover this topic in a separate chapter because of its relevance. Especially for professional services' firms, this is a fine balance.

58% are increasing their email marketing because that typically is the most measurable return on investment. We are briefly talking about this in the automation segment.

The fourth area is an increased spend for social media marketing, which is up there for 57% of the businesses. We cover social media in a separate chapter.

The fifth major area of increased spend is content management with 57%.

I suggest you compare this information with your own numbers and see if you have similar focus areas or where you decided differently and why.

What percentages are spent in which areas at the moment looking at small businesses versus large businesses?

In the area of inbound marketing, it is social media with 18% (7% for large businesses), SEO with 14% (11%), blogs with 11% (3%) and email marketing with 11% (10%).

For the outbound marketing activities, the main areas are trade shows (5% / 17%), paid search (7% / 11%), direct marketing (5% / 9%) and telemarketing (5% / 7%).

I was a little bit surprised about the small amount for paid search because I believe that is a great source for quality leads in a lot of markets. We cover this in a separate chapter.

Let's finally cover some of the major challenges marketers face:
Lack of time is almost always mentioned. Everybody is incredible busy and marketing is often done in a more reactive that proactive way according to a specific plan.
Another major obstacle is related to content. That can be the production of enough content, and content that engages, but also the variety of content.
If you feel that I describe your situation, you will find some ideas in Chapter 10 where I talk about the marketing roadmap.

Let's talk about mobile, which comes up as a top issue, challenge, and opportunity in a lot of places. What I find during my regular talks is that people know mobile is important; but, on the other hand, they don't know how big it actually is. The best way to address this is via relevant statistics.

So, let's start with a funny one. There are 7 billion people on the planet; there are 5.1 billion cell phones or mobile phones, and only 4.2 billion toothbrushes. It clearly shows how important cell phones are and how relevant mobile is.
The next one is even more relevant and important - a really, really important one which really drives the point how relevant mobile is. It takes 26 hours for the average person to report a lost wallet, so roughly one day, and that might make sense to you. The interesting thing is, it take 68 minutes for them to report a lost phone. That is quite a difference between a wallet and a phone, which demonstrates that the phone is the most important item actually that you have.

61% of local searches on a mobile phone result in a phone call. That's a huge, huge number, which shows you how important it is to get things like Google Plus right, how to get your mobile website right, and things like that which you will read about in the book.

We see this with our clients who have mobile-optimised websites. Some are getting a lot of traffic and a very high number of "conversions" - calls or requests. We have a local pizza place as a client, and around 40% of the visitors to the mobile- optimised website are calling to order a pizza!

61% of mobile phone time is spent on apps. So, the whole apps business becomes more and more important. And, again, it can be relevant for professional services' firms to interact with their clients in a different way on their terms and where they spend most of their time.

We have deployed apps "Lawyer or Accountant or Firm in Your Pocket," which puts the firm, literally, into the pocket of your client or prospect. Therefore, the way to get in touch and interact is shorter than via websites and other means.

More than 50% of the users are searching on their smartphone. Actually, the majority of searches are starting on the smartphone and then move sometimes to the desktop depending on availability, and details, and so on, which means the relevance of having everything mobile ready is very, very high. We'll talk about that in the book as well.

This should give a good perspective and view where marketing and, specifically, digital marketing is today.

Clients almost always check you out online, your reviews and ratings, your presence, your messaging.

They'll have a look at you before they meet. They are searching for your services. The number of searches for certain services is steadily growing, and it becomes more and more relevant to be at the right places in the right form.

Two highly critical elements, therefore, are your ads and your online reputation management.

In the next chapter, we talk about how to position yourself and therefore your firm.

CHAPTER 3

Position Yourself and Your Firm!

A fter talking in the previous chapter about what is happening in marketing and, particularly, the digital marketing and mobile marketing world, we now want to talk about how to position yourself.

How to stand out? How to position yourself?

Today's market place is extremely competitive. That applies in general terms. It is true for most business areas, including most services-based businesses, but also other industries just to mention retail, manufacturing, and so on.

But, we want to focus on the services business. So, let's say you're a lawyer, an accountant, or a financial planner. Typically, there are hundreds and thousands of similar firms out there competing for business and positioning themselves. What you might have seen as well is that a few of those firms are actually standing out, and they are seen as the lighthouse, as the authority in the marketplace. They typically demand higher fees, are typically sought after, and don't have to chase clients because clients actually come to them for help.

So, with that, the question is: how do you become an authority in the marketplace today? I want to talk about things that are working today, not yesterday, and, as far as possible, tomorrow. Obviously, I cannot forecast the future; but, at least I know somewhat the trends that are happening right now and that will help you moving forward in the right direction as well.

What I want to talk about are three ways to stand out. I'm covering ratings and reviews. I'm covering the question of how to become omnipresent. And, last but not least, obviously I want to cover what a book can do for you and why you should publish a book.

So, let's get started with the first one: ratings, reviews, and testimonials. You might have recognised, when you search for certain services on the Internet using, for example, Google as the predominant search engine, that sometimes you have these stars attached to businesses. They clearly stand out, especially nowadays where this is not that common yet in many places in the world. So, one of the questions is: how do you get to those ratings and how important is it? Actually, the social proof and what other people are saying about a product and service become more and more important because the online messaging overwhelms people. They're looking actually for what other people are doing and saying so that they have an orientation point. So, it does become more important. Having said that, you have an excellent opportunity to stand out, for example, in Google because not everybody is doing that yet.

It's a good practice today to ask your clients for reviews, for a public review, on Google plus or on Facebook, depending on your business. For some businesses, Facebook is more relevant than Google+. The other item of relevance are testimonials for your business on your website. Again, social proof is important. The way to do this is to ask a certain set of questions, at the right point of time, when you have a good relationship with your client, so that they're actually willing to support you with a testimonial. Furthermore, you can help your clients to write a testimonial draft by saying, "Well, I've put something together, some ideas and you can change it, make something completely new, or whatever you like, and please send it back so I can use that on my website."

By doing that, you actually make it easier for your client to come up with a testimonial.

Another way to get a testimonial is when you are at a presentation or you are doing events. This provides the opportunity, utilising the momentum and the positive atmosphere, to ask for the testimonials and to even consider video testimonials that you record at the event. So ask for testimonials on Google+, Facebook, and in the form of videos.

Many businesses already have a large number of clients, but no testimonials. To overcome this, and to turn clients into testimonials, a structured process can be used.

Clients provide feedback, which you can use as a testimonial. So, that's number one. This really helps you to stand out on Google+, but also on the website. Google will use this and promote your business accordingly.

Secondly, becoming omnipresent. What I mean by that is that you have a social media strategy that supports your presence. You're providing regular content; but then, almost more importantly, you reuse and repurpose existing content. So, let's say you have a book. You could take chapters, or even parts of chapters, for blog posts. You could, then, create podcasts out of that. And you could then create social posts, social media posts, out of that. This reuses and repurposes the content to spread it across various channels.

Then, you start scheduling it for your social media channels - for example Twitter and Facebook. Because of the flow of tweets on Twitter, you can actually tweet the same information and message a couple of times per day without annoying your clients. And, you can automate that process with appropriate tools so that the message or slightly modified messages are going out on a regular but random basis.

The last point around being "omni-present" I want to talk about is retargeting, and this is covered in greater detail in the Ads chapter. Using ads (Google ads, Facebook ads) for your business can be very successful and beneficial. The great thing is you can then start retargeting so that you actually are present across the Internet. You do that by actually putting a pixel out there onto your website or landing page and use this pixel to target those visitors everywhere. A good number of people (up to 25% or more) come back and opt into your list so you can do email marketing and things like that.

The third way to stand out is publishing your own book. Clearly, having your own book can be a very powerful instrument. Imagine you are recognised and seen as an author, as a published author. You could publish under the umbrella of your firm or, for example, all the partners doing something together as co-authors.

I know of people who built complete new businesses based on one single best-selling book because it elevated their status. Suddenly, you get speaking engagements and people start reaching out to you. And, so, it becomes a very strong marketing tool.

Let's say your firm is pitching for a larger deal and you bring your book along to the briefing session and hand it over. This gives your potential clients the opportunity to get familiar with what you are talking about and what you are standing for. Then, when you come back, they already know your background and your story. This means that you can go straight into the content.

Another benefit of a book is that it can give you major media attention across newspapers, radio, television, and more. You can either actively use this or wait until the media is recognising you.

You can even test new business areas. Let's say you want to explore a new field in your business and you want to test the market. You could publish a book about this topic, and see what the response is, and how much interest there is.

At the same time, you position yourself in that segment of the market. You give the book away to clients, to the press, and to radio. This helps you get more attention, more exposure, and therefore you create that authority status.

Of course, you use the book also on your website where you are stating (assuming it's done correctly) that you are a best-selling author. You can provide a PDF version of the book for free, which creates a connection with your prospects.

As you can see, there are many ways that a book can support your business and help you stand out.

To summarise, I spoke about three areas where you can stand out and how to position yourself. Create positive ratings and reviews that are visible, be omnipresent across multiple channels, and pub-lish a book to be recognised as an authority in your space.

In the next chapters, we are now going into the more technical as-pects of digital marketing - everything from mobile, to social media and websites.

When you want to find out more about what a book can do for you and how we can help you with your book please go to http://tiny.cc/yfenbook or scan the QR.

CHAPTER 4

Your Website - Are You Blocking Your Entrance?

There are still a good number of firms and businesses out there who don't have a website yet. These are usually smaller firms, but it shows how slow things have been moving. Even of the firms who do have a website, there is a lot of improvement opportunity.

According to digital marketing guru, Avinash Kaushik, and his digital marketing "Ladder of Awesomeness", an acceptable website is a key component of a digital marketing strategy.

What is acceptable? This is a great question and it is changing constantly. In the not so distant past, it was enough to have a website. Today, this is changing. Usability, responsiveness, and relevance are far more important nowadays.

We conduct regular website audits for our clients - both a more technical audit and a usability audit.

The technical audit is quite straightforward where we analyse a website to identify errors, problems, and other issues that have an impact on the Google rating. This also includes an assessment on a number of keywords to identify if the content is relevant. We, then, deliver a comprehensive report that helps the client to understand how to resolve those issues.

The second part is about usability, and this is an area, which is constantly changing. Interestingly, it is hard to determine right or wrong. Sometimes, the only way to do this is to split test.

What is split testing? You have a number of variations of a site and you direct the traffic randomly to both pages. Then, you analyse the data to determine which options yield the better results.

One of the key things to ensure is simplicity. There is so much information available and clients are easily overwhelmed. It's important that they easily find what they are looking for.

What I see a lot of firms and businesses doing is to focus on their own perspective instead of considering how a visitor and potential client is looking at the site.

The other major challenge is that a lot of visitors are leaving a site quite quickly and are lost "forever". One way to tackle this is to use retargeting. We spoke about that before and will cover it in more detail in the ads chapter.

The other thing you really should do is give something valuable away. This could be a report, a tool, checklists, etc. A great way, obviously, is to give away a copy of your best-selling book. Examples could be: The 10 Things to Do in Case of a Divorce, if you are a family lawyer, or The 7 Steps to Prepare for Your First Property Purchase if you are a property advisor.

In exchange, you get the first name and the email, which then allows you to follow up via email marketing.

What I still see quite often and what works less and less is something like "Join our Newsletter" or even "Join our Newsletter for Free." This did work a few years back, but today people expect something in exchange for their name and email straight away. A great newsletter is a bonus.

Of course, your website should be also easy to navigate - again, from the position of your potential client. You might have your value proposition up in a very prominent way so visitors understand what they are getting from working with you.
What also works usually well is a strong "call-to-action" where you basically tell the visitor what they should do (for example, "Download Your Copy of Our Book Here!").

YouTube videos in your website can actually boost your rankings because YouTube is part of Google and Google just loves YouTube. It is important that you have relevant keywords associated to your videos so those videos show up when people are searching.
Obviously, social proof is important. So, testimonials of your clients should be there, and should be integrated, and should stand out and be very explicit. I spoke in more detail in a previous chapter.

The last, but potentially most important, topic I would like to address is the use of mobile devices when surfing.
Why is it the most important topic? Because more than 50% of all searches are starting on a mobile phone and are often continued on a desktop. But, at least 80% of businesses and firms are not prepared

for mobile visitors, and the risk of losing out against competitors is steadily increasing.

Therefore, you want to have a mobile-optimised website or at least a mobile-friendly one. From our perspective, a mobile-optimised website is the best way to address this trend. This mobile-optimised website goes hand-in-hand with the main website.

You have the standard site and the more simplified mobile-optimised site, which really focuses on key aspects a mobile visitor, expects. This is typically a touch-to-call button, a Google maps integration, and key information about your business.

My recommendation is to get a mobile-optimised website. The second best option is a mobile-responsive one. I would say the downside of the mobile-responsive one is that there's still a lot of content, which people don't necessarily don't want to go through when they're on the go on their smartphone.

For the iPad, I would use a responsive theme. But, for smartphones, our recommendation is always to go for a mobile-optimised website. What I suggest you do is the following: Take your smartphone and access your website. Try to be "neutral" and see how easy it is to get around.

Then, try the same with a number of competitors. I expect that you will come across some mobile-responsive sites and maybe an optimised version as well. If not, you can look at the following sites on your **smartphone**: http://www.smbas.com.au. That's my daughter's business that is helping local businesses to get mobile-optimised websites. Or, check out http://www.khq.com.au , which is an example for a legal client.

What I find during my talks is that most people are surprised about the differences and many have never really tried their own site.

One of the big trends we are seeing at the moment is the so-called multi-screen search. 77% of the mobile searches take place even when there's a computer available. It's really interesting that people start searching on the smartphone and then they'll move to the desktop. It's something happening regularly and you might have experienced that as well. You start searching on the mobile, your smartphone, you search for something, and then move to the desktop to do your proper research on some reviews and so on before you might actually get in touch.

That's why I am sometimes surprised how much businesses spend for flowers at the reception, but they decide not to invest less than $1,000 for a mobile-optimised website to cater for usually more than 50% of their visitors.
Which brings me to the next advantage of a mobile-optimised site versus a mobile-responsive site.

When you are a business with a larger website that is still "old style" non-responsive, the cost of moving to a responsive version can be a couple of thousand dollars.
When you decide for a mobile-optimised version instead, you need less than $1,000. We have a number of clients who decided for this approach.

So, being mobile ready becomes a hygiene factor for businesses. And who else better than the Executive Chairman of Google, Eric Schmidt, can express the relevance by saying: "Mobile is no longer winning, it has already won."

90% of people have their phones 24/7 in arm's length reach, so it is essential to appeal to a mobile user.

If you want to discuss your needs around a mobile optimised website please send an email to contact@totalu.com.au for an initial conversation.

We also offer a very powerful website audit for your website which helps you to identify issues or errors as well as an initial keyword matching of your site. Find out more at http://tiny.cc/yfenaudit or scan the QR code.

With this, I want to close the chapter about websites. I hope it provided some food for thought for your own website or for an upcoming website re-launch.

CHAPTER 5

Social Media for Firms

T his is an introduction into Social Media for Professional Services' firms. I want to cover some highlights and key elements in this chapter.

By no means can this be a comprehensive chapter as social media is probably the fastest changing component of the whole digital marketing movement. Hardly anybody can keep up with new channels popping up and setting new trends everywhere. What is scary about this is the speed those networks are spreading and gaining followers.

To balance this out, there are some major channels to consider and, usually, new channels are often addressing the younger generation. As this book is mainly aimed for professional services' firms, the development is not as fast as for other industries like retail or entertainment.

But, when you develop your overall strategy and then your digital strategy for your firm, I suggest keeping this in mind because elements of your business may require you to tap into new channels - I am just thinking of your recruitment strategy. When you want to attract younger employees, you might find that they are very active on new channels like Instagram or Snapchat.

Let's have another look at the "Ladder of Awesomeness" of digital marketing by Avinash Kaushik and see where social media can be found on the ladder.

Interestingly, social media is relatively high on this ladder, so it is something to consider at some stage of the digital journey. Before you jump in and create accounts on Facebook, Instagram, Snapchat - just to name a few popular ones - you should consider who your ideal client is and where they are active.

I want to put the key criteria on the table straight away - and that is consistency. Starting a channel and giving up, when you don't see the momentum or even the financial results, is not a promising strategy. When you struggle posting every day (or sometimes every second day) and you don't want to use professional support for this, you should not start the journey.

The challenges of Facebook

There are too many dead digital bodies (accounts) out there. And I, too, declare myself guilty of having opened a number of Facebook and Twitter accounts for various ventures. One is a Facebook page (totalu), which has a good number of followers, but mainly because we "acquired" a large number cheaply years ago. The "punishment" is that our posts are hardly seen by anyone due to some algorithms by Facebook measuring the level of engagement. And, when a high percentage of followers are "not real," the level of engagement is logically very low. Even though I have great content on this channel for a year, the engagement hasn't really gone up. The rescue mission would require other activities, but this is no longer a focus area for my business.

On the contrary, my wife was able to build up more than 10,000 likes in less than 12 months. And they are all real "human beings" and very interested in the content. Even then, it is challenging to create a high level of engagement.

To get a better understanding, let's have a look at the largest Facebook pages on this planet (http://fanpagelist.com/category/top_pages/).
The top three are pages from Facebook: Rank #4 is musician, Shakira, with more than 106 million followers, however, less than 500,000 are "talking about" or are engaged. That's less than 0.5%!
Rank #5 is soccer star, Christiano Ronaldo, with just over 103 million followers and almost 5 million "talking about this." That's a nice ratio of more than 4%! So, with one post, he reaches literally millions of people.
Most of the top 100 pages are musicians, actors, and other "mass attractors," but the percentage of "people talking about it" is always low.

My message to you is this: Don't be disappointed when you have 1,000 Facebook likes and only 20 or 30 seeing your posts or "talking about this." Even that might stir up some local interest, raise your firm's awareness, and create goodwill.

One of the questions people ask me is if they should have a Facebook page for their firm. That's why I started with some comments and observations around Facebook.

The answer is that it really depends. When you are in pure "business-to-business," then there are more important channels, which we will cover in a moment.

When you have a more local business, like a law firm or an accounting firm, it might well be worth the effort and investment. Just make sure you are consistent and don't sell. Have a look at Chapter 10 to learn how to create this consistency.

And Facebook can become really powerful when you combine it with Facebook Ads, which we will cover in chapter 6.

Google+, Twitter and LinkedIn - the big gorillas

Let's now move on to the other three gorillas in the social media zoo.

Google+ is a big one. It's so big that we will have to come back in a moment because Google+ is, obviously, the social media of Google and is really relevant. Then, we have Twitter.

Twitter - the powerful real-time messaging system consisting of 160 characters is a true gorilla. There are 200 billion Tweets sent per year or 6,000 per second. This is a staggering number, isn't it?

The power of Twitter is the brevity and the fact that it is real time and searchable, as opposed to Google, which is not real time. You can go into Twitter and check what happens right now! The best use is created via so called hashtags (#YFEN) that are used as a marker to filter out relevant Tweets. Let's say you run a large event and you have screens showing what happens on Twitter right now related to that event. You would define a hashtag (for example #myevent) and everybody's Tweet using this tag could be seen on the screen.

I would like to share a little story answering the question of whether Twitter is relevant for executives as well. I wanted to get in touch with a CEO for a conversation, and the way I was successful was via Twitter. That actually happened more than once. This CEO told me that she prefers communicating via Twitter because she does not have time to read long emails and people should be able to put a key message into 160 characters. Interesting, isn't it?

Let's move on to LinkedIn, which is the largest professional network. LinkedIn is something you should definitely look at and do properly by setting it up in the right way so that you gain LinkedIn credibility. Again, consistency is key, and you want to post on a reasonably regular basis. Valuable content is really important - different from Facebook, which is far more social. All new potential employees, and probably clients, will check you out on LinkedIn. So, that's a base to cover.

Before we move to Google+ - the big unknown child - let me briefly mention the local directories like Yellow Pages, Yelp, etc. They are important and should be covered at some stage. One of the things we help clients with is a "Brand Establisher," which establishes a large number of accounts and secures the digital real estate. This should, of course, go hand-in-hand with a strategy development like I cover in chapter 10.

Now, let's look at Google+. Why is Google+ so important and why is it important to watch out for? As you probably know, Google is the largest search engine, covering far more than 90% of all searches. The term "I Googled something" is used today even if the search doesn't happen on Google. And, secondly, Google owns YouTube, which happens to be the second largest search engine in the world.

Video marketing is one powerful way to move up in the search results.

But, Google clearly likes to support local businesses like you. They
do all sorts of things to promote local businesses who are following
"the Google rules".

One way is to set-up your Google+ account properly in a professional way and link it to your website so that the probability of you being
found increases. Combine this with the generation of reviews and
ratings as discussed, and it becomes a powerful marketing instrument.

You, then, can start posting news about your firm on Google+ as
this will more likely show up higher in search results. Combine this
with regular videos on the corresponding YouTube channel and you
further increase your exposure to Google.

You also need to be a verified local business, which is demonstrated
by the tick under the image. Google can then use your Google+ information and show this when you come up in searches. Of course,
you should have relevant and professional photos on your Google+
account too.

When you cover all these elements, your probability of coming up
on page 1 increases, and it also helps with your Google Ads.

Find out more about our social media optimisation at
http://tiny.cc/yfensmo

So, that covers the introduction into social media for Professional Services' Firms. In a nutshell, set-up your Google+ account and link it to your website and business. Have LinkedIn ready, and then consider channels like Facebook and Twitter.

CHAPTER 6

Google and Facebook Ads - Grow Your Firm With Paid Leads

I n this chapter, we discuss Google AdWords and how you can make it work for your business or your firm. I provide a short overview and talk about some of the key things to focus on.

Google AdWords is an advertising platform that gives you an incredible opportunity for growth in your firm.

There's no better marketing strategy than one that allows you to get solid and measurable results for the growth of your firm, and Google AdWords allows you accomplish just that.

If you are, therefore, looking for a way to really utilise the Internet, generate leads online, and to grow the bottom line of your firm, let this be your guide.

Why Google AdWords?

Television commercials, radio spots, newspapers ads, and billboards have traditionally been the go-to routes for gaining exposure and generating leads for professional services' firms, in addition to referrals of course.

These methods of advertising are all "Interruption Advertising" meaning that you are trying to "Interrupt" as many people as possible with your message and, hopefully, you find a few that are interested.

These methods of attracting the attention of potential clients are antiquated and much less effective when compared to Google AdWords. You will never find a higher quality lead than someone who is in your local area, does a Google search for your services, finds your ad at the top of the page, clicks on it, and one minute later calls your office. This is due to the fact that such a person is more objective to finding and hiring a firm sooner, if not immediately, compared to those who are "interrupted" by some form of media advertisement.

In addition, advertising on Google is 100% completely measurable so you will know EXACTLY what your return on investment is (unlike many other types of marketing like TV and Billboards). This is why Google AdWords is an incredibly powerful tool at your disposal, which takes advantage of beautifully executed timing when delivering ads to people who are already searching for your type of business and delivering transparent lead generation results while you can track exactly what your return on investment is. Google AdWords is definitely one of the great "new" things in the advertising world.

Search engine optimisation, or SEO, which we are covering in a later chapter, is another major but longer-term advertising strategy. It takes a lot of time, money, and effort to organically rank high in search results on Google for any valuable keyword.

Say you're a lawyer that is fresh out of law school. You've opened your practice and are looking to get established. I've got news for you. You're probably not going to rank high on search results through SEO quickly. This is because there are many more lawyers out there who are more established than you are and have been spending thousands of dollars running a strong SEO campaign, and some of them have not even made it to page 1 of Google results. This clearly shows that it will not be easy for you either. Think about this...

Would you rather pay $1,000 per month for a year just to "possibly" get on page one for your desired keyword, and then, if Google changes their SEO algorithm again, you could lose it all overnight without any warning...!! Or, would you prefer to instantly be at the top of the search results for hundreds of different keyword variations (not just a couple of keywords like with SEO) and have new leads and new clients coming in your door right away? Google AdWords is definitely the way to go. This is not saying that I am against SEO.

For those few who make it on top of the search lists there can be a good return. It is just about finding the right mix of marketing activities and being aware of the downsides too.

With AdWords, you can run a simple test campaign for about a week, spend only a few hundred dollars, and see instant results. When that one week test is done, you'll have a ton of data telling you what keywords worked, how many clicks you got, how many leads came in, and how many new signed clients you have retained for the money spent.

From there, you can refine your AdWords campaign even further by continuing to split-test ads and deciding how much you want to expand your campaign. For example, if you spend $1,000 and you make back $5,000, well then the next month you may very well want to spend $5,000 and make back $25,000.

Google LOVES local businesses like accountants and lawyers, and they give you a huge advantage when advertising on their platform by ensuring that AdWords dominates local advertising. First, Google lets you integrate your Google+ Local account with your AdWords account. This means, when people from your local area are searching, your ad will be much bigger than other ads, with your phone number and address right there in the ad. Take time, therefore, to properly integrate your Google+ Local account for your location information to appear in the ad for potential clients to see and click on it. Then, you're going to see a much bigger increase in leads contacting you and making appointments for your services.

Another very important factor to the success of your campaign is split testing multiple ads to find the ones that get you the highest click through rate (CTR).

Most firms that try to do Google AdWords on their own fail because they don't have a good high-converting landing page and/or they have not split tested multiple ads to increase their click through rate. The other good thing is that the more clicks your ad gets, the less Google will charge you on cost-per-click, meaning that it will also be helping you generate more business and save you money on your clicks.

Lastly, you must send AdWords traffic to a landing page. Yes, you need to have one single, simple, easy-to-read landing page that invites the prospect to take action now. These landing pages get the person that clicked on your ad involved right away and contacting you before they get distracted. If your traffic is being routed to your main website, you run a constant risk of that visitor getting distracted by all the different sections on your site and never taking action. Google has become the largest Internet search engine in the world, and now with its AdWords, businesses and firms get a wider platform and the most effective way to market themselves. So, start utilising the power and create new business for your firm.

Facebook Advertisement

We spoke about Facebook in the chapter covering social media.

This chapter talks about an additional element of Facebook - advertising using Facebook.

You might ask what Facebook ads are? If you have a Facebook account, you might have come across posts that are marked as "sponsored." What that means is that somebody pays money so that this particular post is shown in your newsfeed. You might have clicked on one or two and might have taken action based on what you have seen or learnt.

The other types of Facebook ads are the obvious ads on the right side of the newsfeed. They are usually bigger and it's more obvious that these are ads.

Facebook, as Google, is constantly adjusting how they go about ads because this is obviously how Facebook is generating income. So, some of the information in this book might not be 100% accurate anymore, but the principles do apply.

Why isn't it enough to just post on the Facebook page? Let me give you an example to illustrate the problem:

Let's say you have 1,000 likes on your Facebook page (and most firms / businesses are happy and almost proud when they have achieved this).

Now you, or your social media person, post an image with some text. Typically only 5% to 10% - sometimes even less - see your post. So, in this case, somewhere between 50 and 100 people might see the post.

One client has more than 10,000 likes and most posts are only seen by around 150 people to maybe 400 people - so even less.

Personally, I am often asked to "like" pages when people start their business and I usually do. But, as a matter of fact, I hardly see any of the posts - usually none at all.

Why is this and should you still "do" Facebook?

Facebook tries to identify the most relevant and engaging content and push this content. So posts without engagement (comments, shares, and least relevant likes) are not pushed as much as a post with a lot of engagement. The actual formula is more complex.

A certain person will typically only see posts where they had shown engagement in the past.

The main reason is that Facebook Newsfeed is like a fast-flowing river and Facebook needs to decide which drop of water (or post) you are going to see.

And, still, Facebook is the largest social media platform in the world. So, a certain level of engagement typically does make sense, though it might not yield immediate and direct return.

That's where Facebook ads come into play.

Why Facebook Ads can make sense

Most of your clients are on Facebook. That is a statistical fact. Yes, for some industries, the percentage might be smaller, but, Facebook has more than 1.3 billion users. So, your individual client is most likely on Facebook. That's the first reason why looking at FB Ads might make sense.

Secondly, ads on Facebook have a significantly lower price point than Google Ads. It is difficult to give specific examples because a lot of factors go into the pricing of ads.

In Australia, for example, the price for Facebook ads can be as low as $0.15 per click with variations up and down.

Depending on what you are aiming for with Google AdWords, the cost per click (CPC) can go up to several dollars - even $50 and more.

Why this difference and why do both ways have their benefits?

Consider yourself and how you use the Internet. When you are looking for something, you most likely "google" it, which means you look up google.com and type in your search term, for example, "Plumber."

What you get is a list of relevant entries of plumbers and a large number of Ad choices (three at the top, a large number on the right side, and even more at the bottom).

Facebook works differently because you are not searching for a "plumber" on Facebook. You might ask friends if they know a good plumber in your area, but it's not an active search.

But, imagine how much Facebook knows about you, your details, your behaviour, etc.

So, you are able to target certain people to a very detailed level. And, depending which part of the world you are in, it is even more detailed.

Also, Facebook helps you to not only have your ad show up in front of your target group, but it makes sure that it really shows up - different to regular posts as previously mentioned.

So, both channels have a different approach and, therefore, different price points.

When somebody searches on Google for a plumber, then it's very likely that they need a plumber. Facebook Ads are more intrusive and, therefore, require a different approach that guides your prospects through a process or funnel.

Let's look a bit more into Facebook ads and how it works.

You choose your target group. Let's say men between 30 and 35 who are interested in real estate because you are a real estate advisor.

Facebook identifies a target group that fulfils those criteria and you can start marketing to them.

You need to create an ad, which draws attention and makes the audience click on the ad. That can be challenging sometimes and requires experience and testing.

What happens when people click the ad?

Ideally, they are directed to a landing page, which is a simple page with minimal distraction and directly related to the ad. This is a similar concept to Google AdWords. One difference, though, is that the landing page for Google AdWords has the main purpose of getting the visitor to call or, second best, send a request via a form / email.

Because Facebook is much more social, it usually doesn't work well to try to sell something directly. Instead, you give away valuable content or something else that your audience might like and want.

In the case of the real estate advisor, it might be a free book about the 10 key things to consider when investing into real estate.

In exchange, you get the name and email of the visitor. And, then, you can start communicating via email on a regular basis, build trust, and eventually convert into a sale.

How many people click the ad and how many people leave their details?

These are two main KPI's for your campaign. The so-called "click-through-rate" (CTR) of the ad is usually low - sometimes as low as 1%. A CTR of 8% is already very good. And the CTR differs between desktop and mobile - again, something to consider and to plan for.

So, of 100 people seeing the ad, between 1 and 8 are clicking the ad. And you are paying let's say $0.20 per click times 8 is $1.60 for 8 clicks - not bad.

But, the click doesn't make you money. What happens when they come to your landing page? How many people leave their first name and email in exchange for the book we mentioned before?

Numbers vary significantly. Sometimes, only 10% (or even less) are providing the details and, sometimes, you get up to 50% (or even more). This step, therefore, requires a lot of testing and optimisation.

Let's assume we have 8 clicks and 25% leave their details (the technical term is "conversion rate"). You would have 2 new contacts in your database for a cost of $1.60 (or $0.80 per lead). These leads are most likely not immediate buyers, but need to be nurtured over time. What about the rest?

The power of retargeting!

We said we get 8 clicks for our $1.60 and, of those, only 2 leave their details. What happens with the other 6? In the past, those visitors were lost because you did not have a way to reach them again.

This has changed! You can actually identify when somebody hit your landing page but did not leave the details (and therefore reached the thank you page). How does this work?

Imagine yourself doing a treasure hunt with only two stops. You get a stamp at each stop into your booklet with your number on it.

After reaching the finish, you hand over your booklet and you join the party. The organisers don't know which person has which number, so they are not able to know on an individual level who went through both stops.

But, what they can do is identify all numbers who hit only stop 1 and those who reached both stop 1 and stop 2.

Stop 1 is, obviously, your landing page and stop 2 is your thank you page after the landing page. On each page, you provide a unique stamp.

Facebook then knows if somebody was only on the landing page or if they were on the landing page and the thank you page and, therefore, left their details. Now, you can "retarget" only those people who hit the landing page, but not the thank you page, with a different message like "Get two books!".

Why is this relevant for professional services' firms?

A lot of people do market research when they require services and they might not have the time or the interest to leave details. But, when they see different sets of ads from the same firm, they are more inclined to take them seriously and explore the suitability.

This is just one major shift that is happening right now. When you read these lines, there might be new ways of advertising added to the existing.

Let's close the advertisement chapter with a brief overview of the end-to-end process.

End-to-end Process of Advertisement

You have probably recognised that some professional services' firms, like major law firms, use television advertisement and/or radio to get attention, to build up their brand, and to win new clients.

Obviously, this is quite an expensive exercise and it is not for everybody. But, it is also quite interesting to watch and to see how they approach their advertising.

Recently, I watched an ad on TV and looked at the approach this firm took.

Is the TV ad asking to call or to visit a website? I then have a look if the website is mobile-optimised or, even better, if it's a landing page specifically for this TV ad.

Usually, the site is not even mobile-optimised and it's definitely not tailored to the ad.

Given how much money is invested, this is quite surprising and I am certain a lot of money is left on the table.

So, how should you approach your advertising campaign?

This is a brief summary of the approach and is a high-level guideline. Firstly, you need to identify your target group. The more you know about your target group, the better it is. This includes behaviours, needs, wants, psychographics, etc.

You should also check who else is advertising to this group and how you can model what is already working.

You then need to decide if you want to use Google Ads or Facebook Ads (I keep it to those two channels for simplicity). If your prospect is in a situation where they are looking for your services, Google Ads is probably better suited.

If your client can be influenced and is a long-term prospect, then Facebook Ads are a great alternative.

You should also determine budgets and goals for the campaign. The more specific you can be, the better it is.

Now, you need to create the ads - either graphical Facebook Ads or text Ads for Google. It is important to trigger the interest and get the click.

As mentioned, the click needs to lead onto a specific landing page, which is directly related to the ad text. This is probably the most important component of the complete approach. If you don't do this, the likelihood of your visitors or "clickers" not to take relevant action is far higher. This is one reason for the vast difference in click-through-rates and conversion rates like mentioned above.

Once you get the expected result, you need to professionally follow up. In the case of Google Ads, you need to make sure that the person who is taking the calls, for example, is aware of the ads, the content of the ads, and knows how to handle those calls.

For Facebook Ads, it's important to maintain consistency and follow up, ideally automatically, with a series of emails providing insights and value, but also testing the willingness of the prospect to invest (depending on your industry of course).

So, my key message here is to develop an end-to-end perspective of the ad process. That process can break at any element of the chain and, therefore, not deliver the expected results.

When you have questions about how to set up ads on the various channels, get in touch with us. Find out more about our Pay-Per-Click Offerings http://tiny.cc/yfenppc

CHAPTER 7

Automate Where Possible and Personalise Where Necessary

Given the variety of marketing activities and the increasing complexity of the whole subject, combined with the continuous need in organisations to do more with less - or at minimum do more with the same amount of investment - two main questions come up. How can we reduce the cost of operating digital marketing, and how can we reduce the level of manual involvement?

Outsourcing

The first question reminds me of my time at Capgemini, which is a major global consulting, IT, and outsourcing operator with centres in various counties like India, China or Vietnam. When we discussed outsourcing with clients, it was both about cost and the quality of service. Many clients had initial reservations towards centres in countries like India or China. But, regularly, things changed once clients experienced the quality of people and the processes supporting the delivery. I remember one client in particular, a CIO, who travelled to India to visit our centres.

We were already doing work for his organisation on a particular project. He asked the team some questions about the project and the business purpose of the project. The answers surprised the CIO in such a way that he was saying this team knew more about the organisation's goals than most of the local staff.

At the end of the journey, this client was convinced not only about the business understanding of the team, but much more about the quality of services by these remote teams.

At the same time, I have a number of stories and experiences where remote management and delivery was quite challenging.

This situation is comparable with the digital marketing field. Certain services like graphic design, research, or technical development can be delivered at a very competitive rate from various countries. One key success criteria is the management of the delivery process.

The area, which is typically sensitive is everything related to direct client contact. Based on all of my experiences throughout the years, this needs to be well thought-through. An attempt to save cost there can sometimes backlash when not done properly. Outsourcing of call centres, for example, is a very tricky exercise and requires a lot of experience and balance.

But, for many other areas, outsourcing becomes a standard today due to the significant cost reductions.

So, when you consider outsourcing for some of your execution activities - not the marketing strategy - compare various providers and try to get an understanding of their processes, their reporting, and their management.

Automation

Another major trend in today's business world is automation. If you are interested in learning more about automation in general, about the history and current trends, I recommend the book, *Automate This,* by *Christopher Steiner* - fascinating but also scary.

Back to marketing automation. I would say, based on my experience, this is for most businesses - especially brick & mortar businesses - still at the very beginning.

In the online marketing or Internet marketing field, the level of automation is usually a lot higher. I know of a number of businesses that are running more or less on "auto-pilot" with reduced or even minimal manual intervention. Tools available today allow for such business models. And, now, this trend moves towards "regular" businesses.

Again, this chapter is supposed to provide a good overview without going into too much technical detail. I would like to provide a number of examples of what can be done to get your mind thinking about what this could mean for you.

Website

The first step is to look at the website. Are you currently capturing the details of your visitors? When I say "details," I am referring to first name and email - nothing more! There are a lot of studies available regarding the correlation of number of input fields and the number of people actually submitting their details. And the verdict is clear - the less fields, the more contacts.

Some Internet marketers are, therefore, only asking for the email. Most commonly, and this is what we are recommending and using, is first name and email.

Anything else can be asked at a later stage. Of course, you can have a form on your website where you are offering to do something for the client and you, therefore, require more information. But, I suggest complementing this with a simple opportunity to leave first name and email in exchange for something of value.

One powerful piece of content could be a PDF version of your book.

Autoresponder

The software solutions supporting the capturing of details and management of details are called email autoresponders. They are not classical CRM systems, but typically integrate into CRM systems. Their strength is in email management.

Why use an autoresponder? One of the things you can do is set-up automated email once people leave their details. For example, you would send a welcome email containing the piece of content (or a link to it) you promised. So, in addition to being able to download from the so-called Thank You page, people can also download the document at a later stage.

In a next step, you can then create a campaign of emails over a period of time, and this can be weeks or even months, where the system sends out emails with valuable content automatically.

We have a client who has a 10-part series of emails with valuable and relevant content for the readers. And, in case the reader is no longer interested, they just "opt-out" with a simple click. The system manages everything and nobody gets involved.

Let's say you are a property advisor and you have a series of "25 Secrets Every First Time Home Buyer Needs to Know." You can prepare a sequence of, for example, twelve weeks where you send out two emails per week with new secrets. By doing this, you build up credibility and trust with your audience; and, when they are ready to invest, they are more likely to reach out to you. Or, they may get back to you with a question about a content piece, which then can lead into a face-to-face conversation.

All this needs to be set-up only once and then runs automatically.

Of course, you need to balance this with a level of personal attention. But, you could use this as a filter and qualifier and focus on the most promising prospects.

Workflows

The next level is to create complete workflows based on the behaviour of the recipients. Let me give you another example to illustrate. Back to you as the property advisor for first-time homebuyers.

Let's say your second "secret" is a checklist to go through when starting with the property search. The system would recognise who opens the email, and also who clicks to download the checklist. You could then create either a conditional follow up and send a separate email with a more detailed checklist. Or, alternatively, you could get in touch directly and offer a free consultation.

The interactions with the clients are tailored to their specific situation and needs. But, in the backend, it is largely automated and system driven. So, you are able to provide a personalised service without having major overhead.

When you look at those kinds of systems, you need to keep in mind that this also requires a change in the way your businesses and your people are operating. It is a change project much more than a technology project. You should test certain things because, sometimes, it looks great on paper and theory, but reality might be different.

Process Automation

The last example I would like to mention in this chapter is process automation. For most industries, there are certain services, which have a standard process flow. Let's say 80% are more or less identical. The question then is why you cannot automate those processes; thereby, reducing the cost of delivery and also the price point and, thus, take market share from your competitors.

An example would be the Wills process, which is already available online. In most cases, Wills look quite similar. In the case of a "standard" family, variables might be the number of children, existence of property, and some more.

You could set up a process, through a form-based workflow, that elicits the particular situation. If it's one of the standard cases, you could sell a personalised Will for a very small amount of money because there is no manual intervention required.

And for those cases, which do not fit the norm, you could offer a reduced fee because you already know a lot of the information.

Why would you do that?

Well, the trend to automate, where possible, is unstoppable. There will be always innovative entrepreneurs and new businesses testing the boundaries and trying what is acceptable in the market. And once certain things are generally accepted, the masses are going to move there too.

When you are able to participate relatively early on, you can grab part of the market and benefit. This is true especially when you have something of more value you can offer to increase the total client value (TCV).

These are some of the things you can start with to get into the automation space because it is a learning process and it will not happen overnight.

Send us an email (contact@totalu.com.au) or fill out the contact form at http://tiny.cc/yfencontact for an initial conversation.

CHAPTER *8*

The "New" Search-Engine-Optimisation (SEO)

S EO for Professional Services' Firms will, again, only be an introduction to give you the highlights so that you can get started, you can check what you're already doing, and you can adjust what you're doing.

In Avinash Kaushik's "Ladder of Awesomeness" of Digital Marketing," SEO is together with an acceptable website at the bottom of the ladder. So, it is the first step and very important to get started in that space.

Both topics go hand-in-hand to some extent as the website requires relevant keywords covering the keywords of your choice. Therefore, every article and contribution should align and take those keywords into account. At the same time, trying to "overstuff" articles for better ranking doesn't work anymore.

To better understand this, let me briefly explain how Google works and I promise I am won't be too technical.

Please put yourself in the shoes of Google. Let's say that you are the Country Manager of Google for your country. If I asked you, "What are your main goals?", your answer would most likely be something like the following:

"I want to remain the most relevant search engine for my customers (visitors), and I want to make sure that I am providing the most relevant search results for any search. I also want to maximise my advertising income by providing the best support possible to achieve a good return-on-investment to my advertising customers."

Now, consider some of the challenges Google is facing. There are thousands of users out there who are aware of the power of being on page 1 (or even being #1 on page 1 in the organic results) due to the number of "free" clicks you then receive. They will do everything to get there without being necessarily relevant, and there are the strangest and sometimes obscure solutions out there.

So, Google now tries to filter between "really relevant" and "pseudo relevant" - and that's a tough and constantly evolving challenge.

What is the best way, therefore, to approach SEO? Create and distribute relevant content that your prospects and clients love. And do this in "white hat" style, which means you follow Google's rules, versus "grey hat" where you stretch the rules, and "black hat" where you try to find a way around the rules.

Why is being on page 1 (and rank 1) so important? The number of clicks you are getting is very high (numbers vary typically between 20% and 30%). And the top 3 rankings of Google Ads also get the majority of all ad clicks.

But, the challenge is that, for certain keywords, (like family lawyer) there are literally hundreds of competitors. So, it can become very expensive and also a long-term exercise. That's why we address Google AdWords separately as a very powerful alternative.

You can see number 5 only gets 6%, then next 4%, and then it goes down really as number 10 is only 2%. If you spend $700 to $1000 a month on SEO, which is quite common, are you getting the kind of return on investment you want?

Maintaining number 1 is even harder. Basically, you have to do a lot of work, and a lot of relevant work, to keep you up-to-date. It's no longer just the domain name or simple keywords.

The other element I want to mention is dynamic SEO. What do we mean by dynamic Search Engine Optimisation? This approach takes into account the continuously changing landscape and the various channels of content distribution. Then, it takes the firm budget and optimises, on an ongoing basis, the use of that budget. You might combine the efforts "on page" with other content distribution channels like slide ware and a blog. Or, you could create a Podcast, which we cover in chapter 9, that gives you a completely new channel with iTunes.

As a closing comment, I would like to mention that the way search results are presented is changing. Please go back to your role as MD Google. Finding the most relevant content was one goal. And, because most people click one of the top three organic results, it is only really important to make sure that those spots are covered with relevant content. Beyond that, the other goal kicks in, which is making money through ads. To optimise this, you just maximise the space on a page that is related to "non-organic" search. This is on top of the ad results, on the right the ad results, and all Google+ entries. The number of organic results is, therefore, decreased.

Before we move to the next chapter, please take your smartphone - and with 94% probability you have this in arm's reach - go into the browser and search for the services you are offering.

What you most likely will find are two ads on top, which cover more than 50% of your screen, and maybe one organic result. Now, consider that more than 50% of your prospects are searching that way.

I hope that demonstrates both the power and relevance of Google Ads, and of the need to consider the mobile experience for your web visitors.

The next chapter covers some unusual, but also promising, digital marketing methods you might consider to promote your firm.

To get you started with SEO and your most relevant keywords we offer a very powerful keyword research and an initial consultation for free. Please find out more at http://tiny.cc/yfenkw or scan the QR code on your mobile.

CHAPTER 9

Other Forms of Digital Marketing

In the previous chapters, we have covered a lot of content and how you can benefit from digital marketing, what you need to do, and how you get started or continue from where you are already.

What I want to do in this chapter is to highlight a couple of other ways you can leverage the power of digital marketing, either in addition to what you are doing or as a stand-alone element.

Each element is covered with a brief overview to get your thinking started. You can then do some more research or get in touch with me to discuss how this might benefit your firm in particular. The benefits you can expect to achieve are dependent upon whether you are a large, a mid-sized, or a small firm, what kind of budget you have, and what your goals are.

Podcasting

What is a Podcast? A Podcast is either an audio or video stream that is provided via a Podcast platform (commonly iTunes) in an asynchrony way. That means you can watch or listen whenever you want. Your listeners (potential clients) subscribe to your Podcast and automatically receive an update when a new Podcast is available (because it's managed via a Platform).

The beauty of using iTunes is that you have an additional marketing platform with increasing popularity. More and more people love listening to Podcasts - for example during commute times. Therefore, a number of Podcasts are actually 30 minutes duration, catering to a typical commute time. Of course, you need to have relevant content.

Let's say you are a wealth advisor. You could have a weekly Podcast where you share the latest developments and tips from the area of investment.

Or, you are in the real estate business. A weekly update about the local status will be highly regarded.

Or, you are a technology consultant for cloud solutions. You could have a regular interview with other experts or providers.

The opportunities are significant and you can build a lot of good will amongst potential clients. You can also reuse this content or repurpose other content for the Podcast to reduce the production time.

The way it works is that you have a really nice logo, which you put up into the iTunes store. Then, you produce your podcast on a regular basis (a firm schedule is ideal) and then the whole world can access your information.

The content can be downloaded, consumed, and subscribed to. Over time, you create an audience and you become an expert in your specific field. You can also engage your audience and answer questions they are sending in. That works for almost all services areas.

People who are searching in the iTunes store for the relevant keywords will find your Podcast. You, then, add a link to your website and the Podcast so that people can very easily get in touch with you. Why is it great?

Because it puts your message out into the world and then everyone who is interested in what you have to say can consume it at their convenience. So, it doesn't require direct connection and it gives you momentum, especially when you want to stand out and get your message out to create a brand for yourself and your firm.

What is the advantage of a Podcast compared to a blog?

Your Podcast is in the iTunes store, which means everybody using iTunes actually has access. So, when they type in your keywords, you have an opportunity to come up.

It is much harder to find your blog on a website. It is more expensive and it takes more time and more effort.

Of course, the best is to do both and use the same material twice. This also caters to the fact that different people prefer different ways of content consumption. Many people actually like listening. It is also a very personal way of communicating because you are literally "in the ears" of your audience. With this, you then get multichannel coverage.

To get an idea for the look and feel of a Podcast you can check out our Podcast "Digital Marketing for Lawyers". The Podcast has various formats - a webinar as Podcast, a presentation, a simple audio and various interviews. You can find it at http://tiny.cc/yfenpodcast

Webinars

The next topic I would like to cover is webinars.

Webinars are basically online seminars that are very flexible the way they are set up. You invite people to register for a specific webinar. They get an invite and reminders and, once the time has come and the webinar is going to start, they can log in, which works differently depending on the technology.

It is quite easy to join. For most technologies, there is a small download required, but it is straightforward.

Usually, the number of participants is limited depending on the account you are setting up. A standard GoToWebinar account allows for 1,000 participants on one webinar, which sounds like a lot and should be sufficient for most applications.

Recently, a new trend has emerged where the webinar technology is based on Google Hangouts. This sounds very casual, but it offers a technology already available and basically for free. It's still a bit less comfortable and harder to use than GoToWebinar, but it is also cheaper. You can then explore easy-to-use overlays (like WebinarJam) that are using the Google platform, but providing a lot of additional functionalities - from individual registration pages, polls and questions, to an automated follow up and integration into your email system. We have covered some of that in the automation chapter.

During the webinar, the presenter talks to slides in a "1-to-many" model. The presenter's screen is shared so that everybody has the same visual to the audio. You can also share spread sheets or demonstrations of your software. An example would be that a bookkeeper runs regular webinars on how to use XERO (a very popular cloud-based accounting solution) and charges a small amount of money for each webinar.

The systems also support questions and answers or live chats with, and even between, participants. With some platforms, you can even insert offerings during the presentation and much more.

With so many technology options, it is even more important to strategize what you want to achieve with the webinar. The other very important element is the presentation flow. When we work with clients, we use a proven template, which provides a certain flow for most webinars.

Principally, you need to differentiate between purely informative webinars and webinars that have the purpose of selling something at the end. This can be a soft sell or a hard sell, though; this might not work for a lot of the professional services.

The big advantage of webinars are the low cost, the opportunity to reach a lot of people at different locations, the low level of intrusiveness because you can listen to a webinar during a short break, and also the opportunity to create evergreen webinars that you can put on auto-pilot.

Of course, you can reach out to us or to other webinar experts to discuss your specific situation and how a webinar could help your business.

When would you use webinars?

You could use webinars when you want to share relevant content with your audience. Let's say you are in the B2B space, and you organise a monthly webinar of one hour for your clients about a specific topic.

Let's say you are an expert in international IP rights. You could do monthly or even quarterly webinars and invite all your clients and prospects to talk about a very specific topic. You collect questions upfront or you collect questions while you work with your clients.

You might start out with a small group, but this could grow over time once your service becomes better known in the marketplace.

You then turn the webinar into a Podcast, which gives you even bigger reach. In this case, you would have the webinar as a live webinar where people can ask questions and the recording is made available as a Podcast.

You could also use the webinar to convert the audience into clients by sharing valuable content upfront, answering questions, and then offering more advice.

The other model, which can work well is to have an online-based package as an entry product. For example, if you are a family lawyer, you might want to put together a package that covers key aspects of going through a divorce - financial questions, emotional questions, but also legal questions. You could add forms and other valuable information. Once you have this simple program developed, you could sell it without spending more time. And once there are more difficult questions, people would come to you for additional help.

This could create an additional revenue stream and also creates additional leads for your law firm.

Another way to utilise webinars is to answer frequently asked questions. On your website, you could have a membership area where clients have access to your webinars. You could "prepare" them for the main sessions.

Hopefully, that provides some ideas about how you might utilise the powerful tool of webinars. Some people have declared Webinars dead. But, when you provide valuable information, people always listen.

Digital Magazine

Another way of communicating with clients, or also with employees internally is via a magazine.

You may have considered a paper magazine for your clients, but the cost turned out to be prohibitive. Or, you are a larger firm and you are considering alternative ways to communicate with your employees, maybe even across the word. Or, you already have a paper-based version and would like to add more value by making the content available in a different format. For example, you are a consulting firm and you want to provide your clients and prospects the opportunity to read your regular valuable content in the form of a magazine on their iPad or other tablet.

Or, you might not have a paper-based version, but you'd like to send out a PDF version with the latest information, articles, and news. That is nice, especially when it is professionally done, but it is still a PDF. The problem is that, nowadays, PDFs are perceived as lower value because anyone can design a PDF and put something together. So, the perceived value is decreasing.

Therefore, another way to communicate with clients, prospects, employees, or other stakeholders, which is much more exclusive, is to create a magazine - an online magazine.

When I talk about an online magazine, I am referring to an online magazine exclusively in the newsstands, the Apple Newsstand and Google Play. You have those two large major operating systems covering about 95% of the tablet market. The main device for those magazines are tablets; although, you can offer a text version too that can be read on the smartphone.

The beauty of digital magazines is that they are far more affordable today and also easier to produce.

And to the readers, they offer a high degree of convenience because they can read the magazine anywhere on their tablet. It's online and offline available. When the reader is online, you can integrate the magazine with other multi-media content. Imagine you are writing an article about a new investment scheme and then you link the magazine to a calculator on your website. To receive a more detailed analysis, the reader needs to enter their name and email address.

You can offer your magazine for free or you can consider charging a small amount of money for it. From our experience, it is better to give it away for free and use it as a lead generation tool -- assuming you have a good backend.

So, you could take your PDF content, enrich it with multimedia content like videos, etc., and convert it into a magazine. Your clients (or other stakeholders) would have your magazine in their Newsstand. Have a look on your iPad or iPhone and see if you can find the Newsstand. If you can see the Newsstand, whenever there is a new issue coming out, you can notify your subscribers by sending a push notification. This notification lands directly on the smartphone and informs the recipient that new content is available.

Imagine how that would differentiate your business from the competition by offering something like a professional magazine on a regular basis.

At the same time, you open your services to a new client base who are searching for certain keywords. To give you an idea about potential numbers, we are getting 20 to 40 organic downloads of the magazine app for one magazine. And that is per day, and not per week. When you charge for the magazine, only a relatively small percentage will subscribe and pay. But, when the magazine is free, the percentage is certainly a lot higher - up to 50 or 60%. In this case, that might be 10 to 24 new subscribers every day, or about 450 per month, or more than 5,000 per year. Now, imagine how many of those you might be able to convert into clients.

Another way to use a magazine is to drive qualified traffic back to your website from where you convert. Or, you use this to build an authority status in the marketplace. Let's say you are in Real Estate. Instead of doing a Podcast, you could publish a monthly magazine. Or, you could combine the monthly version with shorter weekly snippets with market updates.

As you can see, there are multiple and very powerful ways to leverage a digital magazine for your business. I have only scratched the surface because there are so many other models you can think of due to the multi-media capabilities and the combination of online and offline elements.

To get an idea you could check out our magazine "The Modern Executive" which we have run for a few months. You can download the app (magazine) for iPad / iPhone here: http://tiny.cc/newsstandtme

Let's move to the next powerful tool you can consider for your arsenal - mobile apps.

Mobile Apps

We already touched on the relevance of mobile in the chapter about mobile-optimised websites. You might remember that mobile experience is on level 2 of the "Ladder of Awesomeness." Also, I would like to recap that, for 90% of all people, the mobile phone is in arm's reach 24/7. Mobile Internet traffic surpassed desktop traffic in 2014. Therefore, mobile Internet traffic is more important than desktop Internet traffic, which is an indication of how relevant mobile actually is and why you need to get prepared for the mobile world.

Let's further explore what else can be done to improve the mobile experience of your clients and prospects.

Have a look at your smartphone or tablet and, most likely, you have installed multiple apps. Just think of your banking app, or the public transport app, the weather app, and many more. You might even have an app from your favourite pizza place around the corner to simplify the order process.

Why are people installing new apps? Because they add value, offer certain functionality, or are supposed to make one's life easier.

So, the question now becomes: are there ways you can make your client's life or your prospect's life easier by offering certain functionalities via an app?

One concept we developed is the "Accountant / Lawyer / Firm in your pocket." It is an app that an accounting firm or a law firm or other services firm gives to clients and prospective clients.

By downloading the app, this law or accounting firm is basically in the pocket of the client. So, whenever this person requires accounting or legal support, their first point of call is most likely this app.

Let's say you are an accountant or lawyer, the app provides a number of functionalities to your clients and / or prospects like:

They can record a question and send it to you as the accountant and lawyer from the app. Let's say they sit in a cafe on the weekend and they discuss a situation with their partner. Suddenly, a question comes up. Instead of writing it down or trying to type a lengthy email to you on their smartphone, they launch your app, press "record the question" button, record the question, and with one click it is on its way to you as the accountant or lawyer. For you, the big advantage is that you can process those questions in a consolidated way when you have spare time. You are not interrupted and you can decide when you work on the questions.

Another situation could be that your client / prospect is on the go and they need to send a document to you, as their accountant, because they have a question. Again, they take out the phone, launch the app, press the "scan the document" button, take a photo, and with another click, it is on its way to you as the accountant.

Obviously, there are also touch-to-call buttons, so it's easy to reach you.

Other functionalities could be a calculator, for example, a tax calculator or a finance calculator. Or, you want to provide a rough fee estimate based on certain variables to a potential client. More and more people do online research first before they get in touch with potential partners.

Another application could be to use the app for case management. Clients provide new information, new documents, or ask questions.

Of course, you as the accountant / lawyer would also provide relevant and updated content via the app instead of the website - or through both the app and the website.

This is because another big trend is that mobile apps are replacing websites or at least parts of websites. Think about how you bank from your smartphone. I bet you use the bank app and not the bank website even though the website might be mobile- optimised. Why is that? It's just easier. With one tap, you open the app via the logo, and each functionality within the app is optimised for mobile use.

The same applies for more and more industries. The mobile- optimised website is the entry door for new clients and prospects and the mobile app is used to interact with existing clients. Of course, that is a simplification, but it should demonstrate the trend.

Your clients could also use the app for appointment setting. You could integrate the app with your calendar and your clients would be able to book appointments directly from the app. The app would check availability and would put the appointment directly into the firm's calendar.

The other powerful feature of apps is "push notifications." These are similar to SMS and go directly to the phone screen. Carefully used, they can be powerful. For example, you could send a quarterly tax reminder to your clients. Or, you could send a reminder for an event you are organising. Again, I am only trying to open your thinking and your mind for what is possible.

Another potential benefit of a mobile app is an increase in the loyalty of your clients to your firm because they have you literally in their pocket. They, potentially, see your logo on a daily basis and, when your app delivers value, they use your app designed in your colours regularly.

A different approach for a mobile app would be to have a neutrally branded app addressing a certain topic or area. There is, for example, a divorce app available in Australia. This app provides a lot of relevant information similar to what we discussed in the webinar section. You can offer further information in a consultation session.

This approach will build up a trust level and will make it easier to engage.

As you can see, most of the approaches aim to establish a relationship with clients and prospects as early as possible so that you and your firm are "top of mind." Once the need for the prospect arises, your firm is either "the one" or at least one of the preferred candidates.

Of course, you can also integrate and connect the app to the social media sites, for example, LinkedIn, Facebook, or Google+ as previously discussed. This makes you more accessible for the clients and prospects. All this together provides the opportunity for you to become part of the smartphone of your clients and prospects and, obviously, they would more likely do business with you when you provide those extra services.

Given the still relatively small uptake of mobile apps, this is another way to stand out and differentiate your firm in the market place. Of all the "extra" digital marketing tools presented, this might be the most far-fetched. From our experience developing apps for various industries, it takes time, some creativity, and the willingness to integrate the mobile app with other digital marketing efforts to make it work.

It's not about the app itself. It's about finding ways to make life and living easier for clients and prospects when they use their smartphone or iPad. Given that this space is just developing, there is a lot of room for innovation. But, the best way to benefit from it is to get started and to find out "in the field" what actually works for your clients and prospects. This approach also needs to complement your internal processes and ways of operating. It is a cultural shift, both internally and externally, though the external shift is caused by an overall development of an uptake of technology. Those firms who offer premium services will be winners in the long run. All this digital marketing is about raising awareness and being on the radar screen of decision makers so you can demonstrate the quality of your services.

I want to cover one final piece in this chapter, which is increasingly important, and that is online reputation management.

Online Reputation Management (ORM)

Hopefully, you have not had the need for ORM with your firm. What is ORM and when is it needed?

There is a saying that a certain percentage of customers and clients are "unwanted" or "problem cases." I am being very careful here, but you have probably experienced the same thing. Sometimes, you have a client or customer where you say to yourself, "It would have been better NOT to get this deal."

What if such a customer expresses his or her self online on various channels? Or, even worse, they run a campaign to discredit your firm. It is not uncommon that negative voices have a stronger willingness to express themselves than positive ones.

So, let's say you have a number of negative reviews and ratings. When somebody "Googles" your firm, the initial impression is not so positive or, even worse, negatively tainted.

That is when online reputation management kicks in. It is a service that actively influences your online profile. It can be a lengthy and difficult process, but sometimes it is the only way to get a relatively clean sheet again. How it basically works is that you bury a negative rating, comment, or piece of content under a mountain of positive pieces.

I recently saw another interesting statistic, which said that around 40% of people are willing to travel somewhere else in a city, or even further out or to a different suburb, when they can talk to a firm with positive ratings in local directories. I found that to be an amazingly high number and I was really surprised, which shows the relevance and importance of getting this right.

Impacting those rankings and ratings can be a tedious and lengthy process. And, sometimes, when the negative views are supported or echoed by strong sources or websites, it becomes almost impossible. For example, when one of the big online newspapers reports the negative case, it might be very hard. On the other hand, not being present online has probably more negative impact than running a risk of a negative review. But, the key take away should be to be aware of what is going on and how you are presented online. For example, the marketing manager should be across all online profiles. I have had cases where the firm wasn't aware that there were already profiles established and that they were showing negative ratings.

The other aspect I wanted to cover is your personal profile. I guess you have Googled your own name? What came up? Any surprises?

I know that, when you Google "Michael Alf," you will find a piano player from Germany coming up. I have known of his existence since 1993.

Though I am very active online with many channels, publications, and content pieces, this other "Michael Alf" is dominating YouTube. And, as I mentioned, YouTube is part of Google, so those videos are coming up high on Google as well.

Whilst many of my images come up and, of course, my LinkedIn, Facebook profile, and some others, I do not dominate this one channel.

The other interesting lesson I got from the exercise was that a press release announcing me starting with my then employer is still one of the top entries when you Google my name. This is because it is a trusted news source. Luckily, that is a positive release, so no action is required.

Think about how searches often happen and why the personal branding is very important and becomes, potentially, even more important. Somebody is looking for a service. He gets a recommendation for a particular firm - your firm. They then check out the firm on the web. Is it a pleasant experience on the mobile? Is the site strong and relevant?

During this phase you don't even know that somebody is looking for you. Once that initial check is completed, the individual is researched. What if nothing of relevance comes up when your name is entered or Googled? Or, you have somebody with the same name who is a famous sports person and you are not even showing up on page 1 of Google?

Usually, one of the first entries is LinkedIn. Check the social media chapter. That's why it is important to have a strong individual profile on LinkedIn. Sometimes, there are other entries, like your Facebook profile. You should also see some images if you have some on the net. If you do have images, this is one of the first entries, even if you don't have them necessarily from your own pages. But, if you are quite public - you might be a public figure, or you might have spoken somewhere - those images might come up here.

That is why you need to manage your individual profile in a similar way to your firm's profile.

How can you actually influence your profile and how can you set yourself up so you can convey your messages?

How do you actively manage your profiles so that, when somebody types in your firm's name or your personal name, the things that come up are what you want to come up?

That's why this is different to SEO. With SEO, you want to aim for certain keywords like "best accountant." This topic is more about your personal profile, which is usually not a main search term.

So, be aware and mindful of where your profile shows up online. Actively promote those entries, which are supporting your current cause, purpose, and role. By the way, you will never be able to delete anything what was already online. This is not how the Internet works. So avoid things you don't want to show up, and train your staff how to manage social media too.

Facebook and Snapchat might be great, but be aware that it is a public forum.

To close, I want to suggest that you look at one resource online which might be helpful for your activities.

It's called www.brandyourself.com - a very interesting service that helps you step-by-step through the process and measures your progress. You also get very specific recommendations. I suggest you have a look to see if that's something for you. It won't be very time consuming and it might even be fun.

And if you want to discuss ORM for your firm please get in touch by sending an email to contact@totalu.com.au

CHAPTER 10

How to Get Started OR "Your Marketing Roadmap"

W e have reached the final chapter of the book. In the previous chapters, we have covered a lot of content. I hope you have both a good overview of the most relevant current topics in digital marketing and have some specific ideas on what to implement into your business.

Still, you might say that it's too overwhelming and there is too much to consider, so I wanted to close the book with a chapter about the creation of a marketing roadmap for your firm or business. This roadmap answers the question on how you get started properly.

Core Problems

Imagine a concise and specific marketing plan that integrates your content plan, your products and services plan, and provides a clear guideline what to do when - and, the best, it's oriented at the core problems of your clients.

One core problem of most businesses is an understanding of the ideal customer or client. I am using both terms in parallel here.

Typically, it is a lack of an exact understanding of your client's problems. Most businesses think they know what those problems are, but they might be only 85% right. In the past, this was sufficient; but today, where the market is a lot tighter and more specific, these 85% might not be enough anymore. And a lot of businesses are far away from the 85%; so, for them, it's even more important to get a good understanding.

What I want to address are two things: Today's buyers are overwhelmed by the available information. That's why I kept this book relatively short.

And, secondly, there is a lack of trust in online or digital marketing. This is because it is hard to verify, at least in large part, what is real and what is not real.

You might remember in Chapter 3 we talked about ratings and reviews and how to get those. This is some kind of social proof, but it might not always work, and there's some scepticism even there, especially if it's too one sided and too good.

So, these two challenges need to be addressed. The key one is to understand what is really important, or in other words, what are your client's core problems?

Knowing that you are able to navigate your firm through the challenges of online marketing.

So, my question to you: What if you had a roadmap that told you everything you need to know about who your best customers and prospects are? What their core problems and goals are? What products and services they want? And then question number four, how to market to them effectively?

This is basically what the marketing roadmap master system is doing. It is a four-step approach system and I'll briefly talk you through the steps.

The first step is the customer roadmap. What you do here is you identify the five core problems of your clients. Why five you might ask? Think about the Pareto optimum - typically, five core problems cover 80% of all challenges. People, typically, can't handle more than that as priorities.

The second element next to the core problems is the customer persona. So, exactly who is your client? What do they like? What do they do when they are not working? What is most important to them? Are they in business or employed, etc.?

Obviously, those questions are dependent on your type of business and on the type of clients you have, but I would like to emphasise the value of knowing these kinds of things.

We have one client where we ran the survey and we figured out that the majority of clients were between 25 and 49 years old and a relatively high percentage had their own business. Of course, you can imagine what the impact on the content strategy would be.

How do you find out those core problems?

The best and most reliable way is to go "to the source"! And you go to the source by asking your clients and prospects. This sounds easier than it is, but the results are very powerful.

Challenges of a survey are the duration, the ease-of-use, the incentive to complete, the right structure, and some more.

That's why we use proven tools, a proven approach, and structure and process that increases the number of completed responses significantly.

One client had an overall response rate of 20% of the addressed database. That is a relatively high value, but it's important to get to around 10% at least or have at least 100 responses.

The time it takes for respondents to answer the survey should not be more than around 6 to 7 minutes and a status bar is helpful. Also, it is suggested to put the meatier questions towards the beginning and not towards the end.

The tool we are currently using is Survey Gizmo, but there are other options available too.

Content Roadmap

Step number two is the so-called content roadmap, which then leads into a content plan. Based on the core problems from step one, you now create your content pieces. We suggest differentiating between lightweight and heavyweight content pieces.

Lightweight could be your social media posts, and heavyweight could be, obviously, your book or articles and blogs.

Each content piece can be combined with a story so that clients relate better. And, of course, each piece of content addresses one of the five core problems. Imagine that you don't have any content distribution anymore that is not related to what is most important to your clients.

The other component of this step is to decide which channels to use. Are you using Facebook? Does Google+ work better? Should you Tweet or even Snapchat? Starting from where your clients are and what content pieces you have, you can then determine the channels.

Products and Services Plan

Step number three is your products and services plan. Do you have a consistent products or services map that builds up onto each other? Your products / services plan should start with a free or low cost component. That's something you can sell via your website or during an initial consultation to add value, get a foot in the door, and get clients. This might be a free assessment or initial advice. It's an area where you can become creative because the old-school "free initial consultation" is wearing off a bit.

For us, for example, it's an extensive keyword research which we provide for free, or a website audit which we offer at a low price point. Both add a lot of value to clients and are a good basis for further conversations.

Secondly, you might have an introductory product. This could be something at a lower price point too or it is something, which provides small, but recurring, revenue so you can go back to your clients on a regular basis. One example in our business is a mobile-optimised website I spoke about. It provides significant value for the client, but still has a relatively low price point. Another example is a service which is called "brand-establisher" to secure all your online real estate in a professional way at a reasonable one-off fee. Other examples are a more in-depth assessment of the financial situation of the client, the creation of a "standard" will, and more.

From the business perspective, you need to start looking at the lifetime value of a client and not at the single transaction. Yes, the transaction should be profitable or at least cash flow positive; but, when it helps to transition the client to higher value offerings, it might be worth it.

Thirdly, you have your main core product or service or services. This could be your consulting services, your legal advice, your quarterly and yearly accounting services, etc.

And, finally, you should consider some highly-customised, high-end products and services. This allows you to potentially increase your margins by adding more value to your clients. This could be one-on-one consulting with the managing partner, access to "platinum" services and resources, etc. Of course, the specific model depends on your business.

So, these are the four elements in the product and services plan, which you need to develop.

Marketing Plan

The fourth and last step of the marketing roadmap is the marketing plan. The marketing plan is an integrated plan which answers the questions "what" and "where" on a tactical level. You create a content calendar, which shows you exactly what and when you share content with your audience. It takes away the guesswork and provides a backbone for your business. You still have the flexibility to adjust things and insert more, but it's a great framework and provides peace of mind for the marketing team.

Questions answered are:

How many times per day and per week are you posting on Facebook? How many times are you tweeting per day? When do you post a blog? What are major events?

Different to traditional calendars, this one originates from the core problems of your clients and is not random.

This covers the four steps. Let me summarise the four steps of the marketing roadmap process:

Firstly, learn who your ideal customers, clients, and prospects really are and what their core problems are.

Secondly, create the right content, which will engage them and build that relationship.

Thirdly, develop (tweak and re-package existing) products and/or services, which they will buy and will allow you to escalate along the product and services suite.

And, fourthly, create a marketing plan with the right marketing messages for the right channels that will turn prospects into clients and clients into lifelong advocates.

And this is your marketing roadmap. Please check out more information about the market roadmap at http://tiny.cc/yfenmrm or scan the QR code on your mobile.

Now you might ask what, specifically, is the next step?

The very first step is typically an assessment of where you are in each of the areas - content plan, product and services plan, and marketing plan.

What are your gaps and how do you close them?

And, then, you develop an implementation plan tailored to your needs.

We have covered a lot of ground in a short period of time. But, I wanted to make sure you get a great overview so that you can start planning for your firm and decide where to start and what to focus on. One thing is certain: The development in this space will accelerate over time and it becomes more and more critical to start investing into your digital marketing presence.

Find out more about "Your Firm Everywhere Now" at http://tiny.cc/yfensite

_____

I wish you success and all the best both personally and also for your firm!

Yours truly,

Michael Alf

ABOUT THE AUTHOR

Michael Alf is founder of "Your Firm Everywhere Now" - a digital marketing agency for professional services firms. After working for more than 10 years with a major consulting and IT firm in Europe, North America, Asia and Australia, he decided to start his own business to leverage his experience and expertise.
Michael lives with his wife and two daughters in Melbourne, Australia.

Disclaimer

"Your Firm Everywhere Now" is a brand of totalu Pty Ltd. (totalU).

No warranties

The information in this book are provided "as is" without any representations or warranties, express or implied. totalU makes no representations or warranties in relation to the information and materials provided in this book.

Without prejudice to the generality of the foregoing paragraph, totalU does not warrant that:

- the information in this book is complete, true, accurate or non-misleading
- Nothing in this book constitutes, or is meant to constitute, advice of any kind.

Limitations of liability

totalU will not be liable to you (whether under the law of contact, the law of torts or otherwise) in relation to the contents of, or use of, or otherwise in connection with, this book:

- for any direct loss;
- for any indirect, special or consequential loss; or

for any business losses, loss of revenue, income, profits or anticipated savings, loss of contracts or business relationships, loss of reputation or goodwill, or loss or corruption of information or data have reached the final chapter of the book. In the previous chapters, we have covered a lot of content. I hope you have both a good overview of the most relevant current topics in digital marketing and have some specific ideas on what to implement into your business.

16763927R00057

Printed in Poland
by Amazon Fulfillment
Poland Sp. z o.o., Wrocław